Other titles in the series:

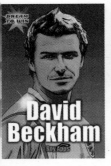

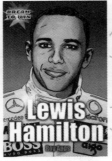

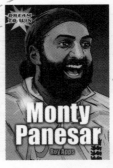

978 0 7496 8232 3   978 0 7496 8233 0   978 0 7496 8235 4   978 0 7496 8234 7

Olympic Gold – available from Summer 2009

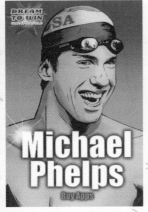

978 0 7496 9028 1   978 0 7496 9195 0   978 0 7496 9196 7

First published in 2009 by
Franklin Watts
338 Euston Road
London NW1 3BH

Franklin Watts Australia
Level 17/207 Kent Street
Sydney NSW 2000

Text © Roy Apps 2009
Illustrations © Chris King 2009
Cover design by Peter Scoulding

A CIP catalogue record for this book
is available from the British Library.

ISBN: 978 0 7496 9027 4

Dewey Classification: 796.358'092

1 3 5 7 9 10 8 6 4 2

Printed in Great Britain

Franklin Watts is a division of Hachette Children's Books,
an Hachette UK company.
www.hachette.co.uk

Andy Murray

Roy Apps

Illustrated by Chris King

EDGE
FRANKLIN WATTS
LONDON•SYDNEY

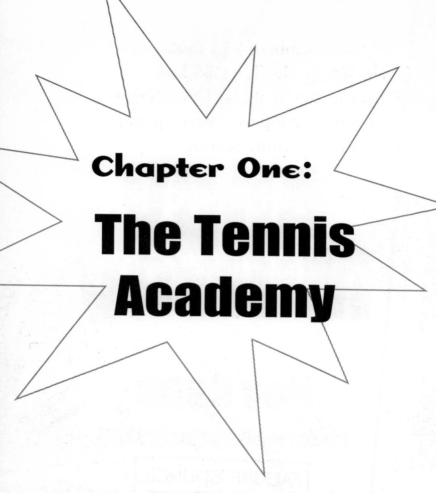

Chapter One:

The Tennis Academy

The Great Britain Under-16 tennis team had
done really well. They'd reached the finals
of the European Team Championships.
But now they had lost their match to Spain.
Most of the players weren't too depressed
about their loss.

Only one member of the team looked really fed up. He didn't like losing. Especially not finals. He had a dream of becoming a top world-class player. His name was Andy Murray.

After the tournament, Andy got talking to one of the Spanish players, a boy he had known for two or three years, who was called Rafa Nadal.

"Who do you practise with, Andy?" Rafa asked.

Andy shrugged. "Anybody I can find," he replied.

"I practised with Carlos Moya last week," Rafa said.

"Carlos Moya? But he's in the World Top Ten!"

"And don't I know it," Rafa sighed. "Do you know, all the times I've played him I've never taken one set off him!"

"So why do you play against him?" asked Andy.

"Because playing guys like that is the only way to become a world-class player," Rafa replied.

7

When he got home, Andy told his mum: "In Spain, Rafa practises with Moya! And it's sunny all day! And he hardly ever goes to school! How can I achieve my dream of becoming a world-class player, when I'm living in a country where it rains all day and I have to practise tennis with my mum?"

Somehow his parents and grandparents found the money so that Andy could take up the offer of a place at the Sanchez-Casal Tennis Academy, at Barcelona, in Spain. He was thrilled. But he had a shock on the first day, when he got his daily timetable, which read:

9.00am – 12.00pm	Tennis training on court
12.00pm – 1.00pm	Fitness Training
1.00pm – 2.00pm	Lunch
2.00pm – 4.00pm	School
4.00pm – 6.00pm	Tennis
6.00pm – 8.00pm	School

Being a student at the Sanchez-Casal Tennis Academy was going to be hard work. Andy didn't mind, though. The only downside was that despite what Rafa Nadal had told him, you still had to do school lessons.

At the weekends, Andy and his friends from the Tennis Academy would take the bus into the city and go to the shops, the cinema, and the go-kart track.

Andy's tennis improved, too. He went on tour to South America. He won the Canadian Open Junior competition, beating the Wimbledon Junior champion 6–2, 6–1.

Andy felt good. Everything was going just right.

Chapter Two:

Loser!

A hot Spanish sun beat down on the tennis courts.

Match point.

Andy's opponent bounced the ball carefully three times on the clay before throwing it up into the air to serve.

There was a thud as his racket made contact with the ball.

There was a puff of dust as the ball thumped into the clay on his opponent's side of the net.

Andy dived at full stretch in a desperate attempt to return the serve. The ball hit the top of his racket and bobbed harmlessly away over the white lines and out of the court.

His opponent clenched his fist, punched the air and ran towards the net.

Andy shook hands with him then, muttering under his breath and banging his racket in anger and despair on the ground, he skulked back to the changing rooms.

Andy's face was hard and set. It was the face of someone seriously thinking about giving up the game of tennis. And who could blame him? He had just been thrashed. He wasn't just a loser. He was a 6–0, 6–0 loser.

He slumped down on the bench in the changing rooms. His knee hurt like mad. Something was wrong. He'd told the physio about it, but the physio had just said: "Put some ice on it and try to give it a bit of a rest now and then."

But he knew he had to get it seen to. And he had to start winning again. Quickly.

Before his dream of becoming a world-class tennis player disappeared forever.

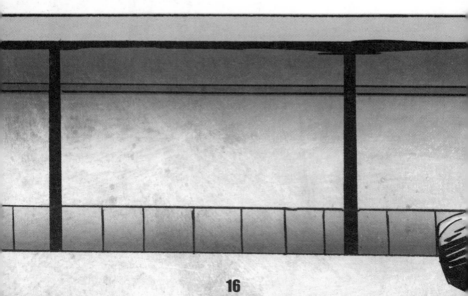

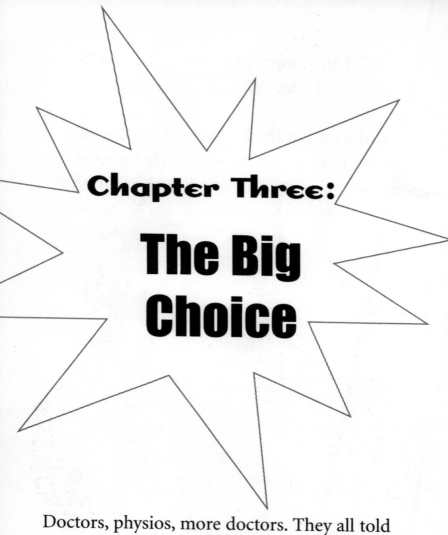

Chapter Three:

The Big Choice

Doctors, physios, more doctors. They all told Andy to rest. There was nothing wrong with his knee.

But Andy knew something was wrong. "I don't believe them," he told his mum.

"OK," Andy's mum said with a sigh, "we'll visit one last doctor."

The doctor put the X-rays he had taken of Andy's knee up on the screen. He frowned and scratched his chin. Andy waited for him to speak, to say like all the others had said: "There's nothing wrong. Just rest the knee."

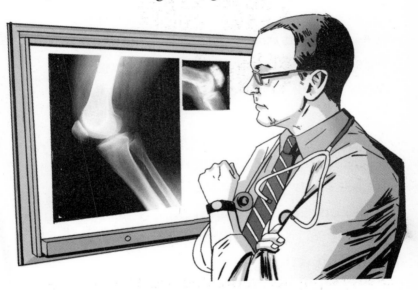

Eventually, the doctor turned round to face Andy. "You've got a problem," he said. "Part of your kneecap hasn't grown properly. You don't need surgery, but you certainly need a lot of rehab."

Andy did rehab every other day, using upper body weights. His knee was too bad for him to be able to stand on the tennis court and hit a ball, so he sat in a wheelchair and practised his shots from there.

By the summer of the following year, 2004, he felt ready to play tennis again.

His opponent in his first match was Jimmy Wang, ranked number 200 in the world. Andy ran on to the court, ready to go.

And go, he did! Twice he broke Wang's serve, cracking high-speed returns down the line. He felt really good, as if now, at last, his problems were all behind him. At 3–1 up in the first set, he ran along the baseline to reach a difficult return.

Suddenly, he slipped. He fell in a heap on the grass.

He couldn't get up. He'd injured his hip. Angry and frustrated, he had to retire hurt.

Out of competitive tennis again, with another injury, Andy had plenty of time to think. Should he quit or should he carry on and try to achieve his dream of becoming a world-class tennis player?

It was a tough choice.

If he carried on, it would be hard work; he might get another injury; he might not even make the grade. Perhaps it would be better to give up now.

Then he remembered how, a few years ago, he'd had to make another big decision about a career in tennis.

Chapter Four:

Chance of a Lifetime

It was when Andy was thirteen. In those days, he played more football than tennis. Sometimes he played as a striker, sometimes as a midfielder. His team was Gairloch United. It was well known for producing high-quality young footballers, and professional scouts often visited their matches.

One day, after a match, Andy was settling
down for a bite to eat in his local
McDonald's, when the coach came up to
his table.

"Mind if I join you, Andy?" the coach said.

Andy shrugged.

"There was a scout from Rangers at the
match today, and he's just had a word with
me. He'd like to offer you a place at the
Rangers Football Academy." The coach
grinned with pride. "Well, what do you say?"

Andy didn't say anything. He couldn't. His mouth was full of burger. When he did manage to speak, all he said was: "Wow. That's great!" but what would any person say if they were made an offer like that? Rangers were one of the two biggest clubs in Scottish football.

Andy's family were thrilled, too, especially his grandpa. He had been a professional footballer with Hibernian and Stirling Albion.

"I hope Rangers pay you more than Stirling Albion paid me," he chuckled. "Do you know how much I got?"

"Eight pounds a week," replied Andy, who had heard the story many times before.

"Eight pounds a week," said his grandpa.

But Andy kept going to tennis practice. He was really enjoying himself. He was about to serve when he saw his dad by the gate, waving to him.

"Come on Andy, you've got to go to football," his dad called.

Andy walked across to his dad. "I'm just going to start the next match."

"But I thought you wanted to play football?"

"I do! But I want to play tennis, too!" said Andy.

"If you want to play professionally you need to choose," his dad said. "Football? Or tennis?"

Sometimes, choices are hard. But at that moment, for Andy, it was almost a no-brainer. His dream was to become a world-class tennis player.

"Tennis," he said, straight away.

"OK," replied his dad. "I'll ring Rangers and tell them."

It was seven months before Andy even looked at a football again.

Chapter Five:

A Hard Road

Back in Spain, Andy had to decide again: should he do rehab to recover from his latest injury? Or should he give up professional tennis? It didn't take him long to make his decision this time, either.

Tennis was still his life. Becoming a world-class tennis player was still his dream. He would try and recover from his latest injury.

When he told his mum she said: "Oh, that's good. Because I've found you a brilliant physio."

Somehow, Andy got fit enough to be playing again a few weeks later. He even played in the Wimbledon Junior competition.

But he lost in the third round. He was too weak after his injury.

He heard coaches and commentators saying that he was injury-prone, that he lacked concentration, co-ordination and strength.

Andy was bitterly disappointed. He ambled out of the All England Club. He wondered if he'd ever come back to Wimbledon. If he did, it would have to be as an adult. He'd be 18 next birthday, too old to be a tennis junior any more.

Behind him, he could hear the cheers from the crowd watching the big Centre Court match. His dream of becoming a world-class tennis player seemed a long way off.

Andy practised, trained and played as much as he could. It was the only way to get stronger; it was the only way to become a better player.

He won the US Open boys' title and turned professional the following year. He played as much tennis as he could. He won matches and he lost matches.

Then in June 2005, he played at Queen's Club in order to prepare himself for his first ever Wimbledon as a senior pro.

He played well in the first two rounds. But in the third round he twisted his ankle and hobbled off.

Andy's physio worked wonders and got him fit for Wimbledon. But that twisted ankle meant he hadn't had time to play any preparation matches. He hadn't even had time to practise.

Was this the time to be entering your very first Wimbledon as a senior professional, Andy wondered?

But if he withdrew now, his dream of becoming a world-class player would be over.

Chapter Six:

Wimbledon 2005

It was incredible, really, thought Andy, as he stepped out onto Court Two for his first match at Wimbledon as a senior pro. A few weeks ago he had been playing in front of a crowd of five people at a tournament in Germany. He remembered the locker room there. It had been small, dark and smelly. It had reminded him of his old school changing rooms.

Nobody had taken any notice of him on his way in. Why should they? They had no idea who he was. He was just another tennis player, barely 18 years old, trying his luck in his first year as a professional. He was ranked 317th in the world.

Andy's first round opponent was George Bastl of Switzerland, a player ranked much higher than he was. But then everyone seemed to be ranked higher than Andy Murray.

Not many people were watching as the umpire called "Play!" and Andy threw the ball up to serve. He should have felt sluggish after missing so much practice, he thought. But he didn't. He felt strong and confident. He felt he had a chance of winning the match.

By the time Andy had taken the first set 6–4 and was a break up in the second, he saw that the crowd was growing.

By the time he took the second set 6–2, the Court was packed. A buzz of excitement ran round the whole place; a young British player was on the brink of causing a major upset! Could he do it?

In the third set, with every point Andy won, the crowd cheered and clapped. Each time he served, they became absolutely hushed.

By the eighth game, it was match point with Andy 5–2 up. Andy made a hard, fast return from the baseline. The ball thudded onto the grass, just out of George Bastl's reach.

"Game, set and match to Murray; 6–4, 6–2, 6–2!" called the umpire, but nobody could hear him over the roars and cheers from the crowd.

Andy ran to the net, shook his opponent's hand, then punched the air with his fist.

Against all the odds, he had won his first match as a senior pro at Wimbledon.

He was moving up the rankings.

Becoming a top-ten tennis player was no longer just his dream.

It was his next goal.

Fact file
Andy Murray

 Full name: Andrew Murray

 Born: Dunblane, Scotland – 15 May 1987

1990	Aged 3 – Andy starts playing tennis. He begins by playing with sponge balls indoors, before moving on to Swingball
1992	Aged 5 – plays his first tennis tournament (under-10's) at Dunblane Sports club
1996	Survives the Dunblane Massacre, in which 16 children and their teacher were killed at his primary school
1999	Wins the prestigious Orange Bowl junior event in Florida, USA
2004	Wins the US Open boys' title
2005	Aged 18, youngest British player in the top 100 since 1974
2006	1st ATP Tour title in the SAP Open in San Jose, coming from behind to beat former world number one Lleyton Hewitt
2008	August – wins his first Masters Series shield in Cincinnati, defeating Novak Djokovic in the final 7–6, 7–6
2008	September – reaches first Grand Slam final at the US Open, defeating Rafael Nadal for the first time. Loses final to Roger Federer
2009	January – wins Abu Dhabi World Tennis Championships, beating Rafael Nadal in the final, 6–4, 5–7, 6–3
2009	February – wins the World Tennis Tournament in Rotterdam, the 10th title of his career, beating Rafael Nadal 6–3, 4–6, 6–0 in the final

Chris Hoy

Edinburgh's largest cinema was packed with people. Everyone's eyes were fixed on the giant screen. The film had nearly finished. The hero, a boy called Elliot, and his friends were pedalling away on their BMX bikes, trying like mad to escape from the police and other grown-ups. Then, suddenly, they took off and were flying through the air on their bikes with E.T. A great cheer went up from the cinema audience.

Every kid in the world who saw the film *E.T.* wanted to be a BMX rider. The group of friends from Edinburgh who had gone to see the film was no different. They walked back home discussing ways to get their parents to buy them all BMX bikes, including the tallest of them, a blond boy, whose name was Chris Hoy.

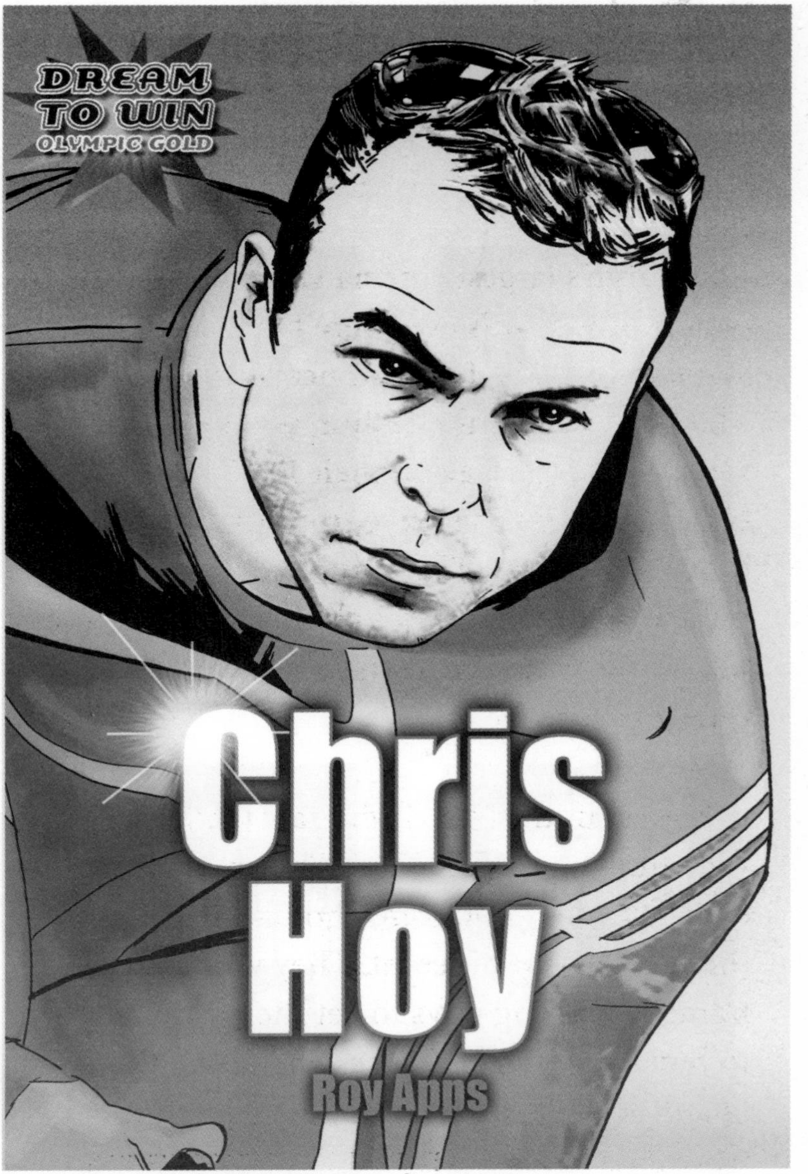
DREAM
TO WIN
OLYMPIC GOLD
Chris
Hoy
Roy Apps

Also by Roy Apps,
published by Franklin Watts:

978 0 7496 7057 3

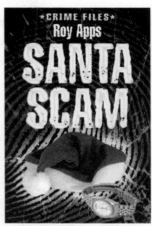

978 0 7496 7056 6

978 0 7496 7054 2

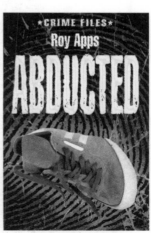

978 0 7496 7053 5